# Mastering the
# Leisure Induction

A Powerful, Efficient and Simple Approach
to the Induction and Deepening of Hypnosis

# Mastering the

# Leisure Induction

## by Graham Old

A Powerful, Efficient and Simple Approach to the Induction and Deepening of Hypnosis

Published by Plastic Spoon

First Published – September 2014

## Preface to the Series

Since starting the website howtodoinductions.com, I continue to be grateful for the number of people who have expressed enthusiastic thanks for its existence. It seems that people have appreciated its explanations and commentary as much as its presentation of various inductions.

This lead me to wonder how many books took the time to focus on hypnotic inductions in the same kind of way. The answer was not many at all! Some books will discuss the nature of inductions, or delve into the theory. A few will share thoughts on a handful of different inductions. However, it remains true that there are very few works which unpack an individual induction, discuss what may be happening *within* the techniques involved, cover any potential difficulties the hypnotist may encounter and go on to offer alternative variations.

Thus was born the idea for *The Inductions Masterclass* series. Our hope is that this series will fill a vital gap in the Hypnosis education market.

In style, the series is a fairly unique experiment. We are aiming to replicate the level, detail and quality of information you will receive at a live training. We aim to anticipate questions from the Floor, as well as handle natural diversions and meandering discussions.

Yet, more importantly, The Inductions Masterclass series will take one induction each and then use that induction as a training tool for learning about hypnosis and hypnotherapy in general. In effect, each book will function as a doorway into the wider world of hypnosis, whilst providing valuable insights into the workings of the induction in question.

As with all of our products – and our live training – our

aim is to teach deep theory and practical knowledge in a refreshingly clear and accessible way.

To set the tone and start us off, I am delighted to introduce you to the principles and practice of the Leisure Induction.

## Acknowledgements

It would be unthinkable to me not to express my gratitude to Jon Old, who – aside from being an unmatched master with the Leisure Induction – is an accomplished therapist, trainer and full-time sounding board for my ideas.

Many thanks are due to Stephen Brooks, from whom I first learned a version of this induction. It has kept a special place in my heart ever since.

## All Rights Reserved

## Disclaimer

This work is meant as nothing more than a discussion of one way to employ revivification in hypnotic inductions. It offers a model for consideration, investigation and conversation. This approach is based upon our own clinical studies and is being made public for the purposes of research and development. It is not meant as a replacement for proper training in hypnosis or psychotherapy.

Please be aware that any experimentation with the ideas presented in this document is undertaken at your own risk and responsibility. At all times when practicing hypnosis, it is your responsibility to ensure that you comply with the laws and regulations of your home country, region, state or territory.

# Contents

GRAHAM OLD

# Introduction

In *Trance-formations*, Richard Bandler and John Grinder state that, 'The easiest of all inductions is to ask your client if she has ever been in a trance before.'[1] Similarly, Michael Yapko states that, 'Making use of the client's previous experience with hypnosis, whether formal or informal, is one of the easiest yet most effective induction and deepening processes.'[2]

I could not agree more. For that reason – and a host of others – the Leisure Induction that you will learn in these pages is one of my favourite ways to guide someone into hypnosis. It is simple, powerful, reliable and enjoyable, for all involved.  However, one of the things that I particularly like about it is that it can work just as effectively without any mention of previous 'trance' or hypnosis at all.

In fact, if I am ever asked about Conversational Hypnosis and asked to give a demonstration, it is more

---

1

Bandler, Richard & Grinder, John (1981). *Trance-formations*. Utah: Real People Press. p.49.

2  Michael Yapko (2003). *Trancework*. 3rd ed. New York: Routledge. p.315.

often than not a version of the Leisure Induction that I turn to. To the amazement of any onlookers, what begins as a simple and natural conversation appears to morph into an experience of hypnosis before their eyes.

Within the pages of this book, we will present the Leisure Induction as a microcosm of the whole field of hypnosis and hypnotherapy. That is, in mastering this one induction you will learn some of the core skills required to be a good hypnotist and will absorb some of the fundamental principles of effective therapeutic hypnosis. On top of that, you are about to see that 'the easiest of all inductions' is also one of the most powerful and useful that any hypnotist would want to have in their toolbox.

Having explored the benefits of learning this induction, we will start with a real transcript from an actual session, where the Leisure Induction was used. This will demonstrate a typical example of the induction in practice. Although later pages may make the process appear complex and outside of the reach of all but expert Hypnotists, if you follow the structure of this book you will find yourself able to perform the induction within just a few pages. As you carry on reading, you will learn nuances and skills that enable you to expand the induction and apply it effortlessly and effectively in all manner of situations.

The first transcript included lasted no more than 5 minutes and is typical of the Leisure Induction. So, we will begin with this and then de-construct it, in a thorough, straightforward and user-friendly manner.

We will then move on to look at some of the core principles at work in this induction, particularly utilisation.

These Core Principles – as well as the later Core Skills – are named as such not simply because of their importance to this induction, but also because of the valuable role they play in hypnosis generally. As will be common across *The Inductions Masterclass* series, the reader will find that attention to the details of the particular induction under discussion will pay dividends in their wider hypnotic practice.

At this point, another transcript will be discussed, demonstrating the points just taught. This means that if you practically follow what is being taught at each step, you will be able to perform the induction almost from the beginning, whilst  growing in knowledge and skill as you proceed.

The core principles will be followed by core skills, with yet another real-world example. This will include a valuable discussion of the physical and verbal signs that tell you someone is going into hypnosis,  sometimes referred to as 'the minimal cues of trance'. They may be considered as basic skills of the advanced hypnotist.

We will then turn our attention to the question of 'deepening' the hypnotic experience. Once again, we will provide a transcript demonstrating what is being taught at each step.

The book ends with a trouble-shooting section and Frequently Asked Questions, followed by detailed appendices. Our intention is that readers will feel as prepared as they do informed and quickly find themselves in a position to confidently use and enjoy the Leisure Induction.

There are numerous exercises to be completed

throughout the book, to practically reinforce the information presented within. It is suggested that you take part in these with what teachers of Zen call a 'Beginner's Mind' – humbly enjoying the experience of learning and experiencing something new, without having to get frustrated with how competent you may or may not yet be. Mastery is the result of knowledge, dedication, practice and time. You focus on those and it will take care of itself.

## Terminology used

Throughout this book you will find us referring to 'trance' and at times using terminology such as 'subconscious', deepening, being 'under' hypnosis and so on. Please bear in mind that these are phenomenological descriptions, merely meant to convey what the hypnotee may be experiencing. We are not endorsing any particular interpretation of hypnosis, or taking sides in the perennial debates over the nature of trance or the existence of a special hypnotic state.

For more on our experiential model of hypnosis, which fits comfortably with all the major schools of Hypnosis, see our Book, '*The Anatomy of Inductions*'.

**EXERCISE:**

Before we begin, take some time to think of your own preferred means of unwinding.

What is it that you like about that activity?

Why do you value it?

Next, think of the other activities that you may take part in, to relax, unwind or 'escape' the pressures of every day life.

Do these activities share any common characteristics? Can you see what it is that you value you about them?

Imagine that you had 60 seconds to sell your preferred means of unwinding to someone else? What would you say? How would you present it in the most compelling way?

GRAHAM OLD

# Why Learn The Leisure Induction?

There are a number of reasons why you might choose to learn and implement the Leisure Induction.

Some people value the way that it can be used covertly as well as overtly. Some people like the way that it can seemingly achieve deep 'states' of hypnosis in a relatively short space of time. Conversely, others appreciate the unique way that it proceeds at a comfortable pace for both practitioner and hypnotee. However, we have not chosen to focus on any of those reasons here.

Instead, in this chapter we will present some of the main reasons that we believe you will find this to be an invaluable induction to have in your toolbox. This is invariably one of the first inductions that we will teach to new hypnotists and experienced therapists alike. Here are some of the reasons why.

## Versatile induction

The Leisure Induction is a versatile tool that you can adapt and use in various ways, depending on the situation you find yourself in. It can be used on the streets, in impromptu settings, just as comfortably as in the clinic, for therapeutic purposes.

Appendix A presents a number of different ways to begin the induction, precisely because it may be being used in a variety of settings.

## No scripts are necessary

Contained within the Leisure Induction are principles and skills that will enable you to hypnotise people anywhere and everywhere, with your only script being the person in front of you.

In fact, an integral element of the induction is listening to the client in front of you and allowing your natural interaction to guide the conversation.

## Empowers your client to experience hypnosis through prior experience

At the core of the Leisure Induction is 'revivification' of a prior pleasurable trance-like experience. There is a fundamental therapeutic purpose to this, which is to teach people that they already have within them the ability and resources to enter into an hypnotic experience. This means that any time you use this induction to hypnotise someone, you have already laid an important foundation for teaching self-hypnosis, performing re-inductions and therapeutically practicing ego-strengthening.

Appendix D offers some brief thoughts on how you might find the approach taught in this book to be particularly useful with analytical or critical clients.

## It is enjoyable and familiar

Unfortunately, anyone who uses hypnosis will still at times have to deal with the aftermath of a previous generation's image of Hypnotists. This is in no small part down to continued media representations of a Hypnotist controlling and manipulating innocent and susceptible victims.

It can be frustrating and occasionally time-consuming to have to allay the fears of those in front of us, who may be willing yet terrified to experience hypnosis. The Leisure Induction is beautifully suited to such occasions. At the heart of the induction is a re-living of a previous pleasurable experience, so there is no concern or fear over returning there. In fact, the client looks forward to it! Additionally, as it is the client's own memory they are returning to, there are no hidden surprises or nasty shocks to anticipate. I can honestly say that I have never had a client displaying an abreaction during this induction, or in sessions following its use.

## Minimalistic

The Leisure Induction can function as an example of practically content-free therapy. It is always a pleasant surprise when clients feedback how powerful and valuable it was for them to experience this process, regardless of any explicit therapy which may or may not have happened.

## Simple and Effective

The Leisure Induction uses simple communication skills that 90% of us use on a daily basis and will be more than familiar to therapists. As implied in the introduction, the various transcripts within this book tend to unpack the induction with  progressively deeper levels of detail and complexity. Nevertheless, it really can be as simple as the basic process below suggests.

**EXERCISE:**

Try to explain your favourite leisure activity to someone solely by talking about how it makes you feel and the effect it has on you.

See if the person you explain it to can guess what your activity is, even without you describing it externally (i.e. without saying what the activity would look like to someone watching you take part).

Then, swap places and invite them to explain their favourite leisure activity, simply by telling you about the way it makes them feel.

GRAHAM OLD

# The Basic Process

1. Ask your client to tell you about an activity or pass-time that they enjoy

2. Ask questions to gain more information: what, when, where, why, how, etc.

3. Repeat back to them what they have said to you

4. Help them feel the memory in the present moment

5. Move from an external focus to an internal one

6. Say what you see

7. Let the client go into hypnosis

**EXERCISE:**

Using the Basic Process as your framework, find a practice-partner and engage them in a conversation.

Do not focus on trying to induce hypnosis, or achieve trance, or anything like that. Instead, simply have a conversation with them.

Be interested in what your partner has to say, particularly when they mention – explicitly or implicitly – what it is that they value about their leisure activities.

# The Initial Transcript

Let's turn now to look at the first transcript of this induction in action. And buckle-up, because from this point on you may never approach hypnosis in the same way again.

The aim of the induction is to simply find something the client loves doing that takes them away from the everyday activities of life. It is not necessary to explicitly connect this to hypnotic trances, but some people like to use their pre-talk to discuss the similarities between naturalistic trances and hypnosis. In the example below, there was no pre-talk and the induction began the minute the client sat down. All you really need to do is get them to recollect something they love doing that is solely about them being happy and enjoying themselves. This could be anything from lounging on holiday by the pool, to fishing by a lake, to a massage or even working-out at the Gym.

Hypnotist: "So tell me a little about yourself. Tell me, for example, what is your favourite leisure activity?"

Client: "I love walking on the hills. I love being

25

outside in the fresh air."

H: "Oh, you like walking on the hills and being in the fresh air?"

C: "Yeah, its great."

H: "Where do you do this?"

C: "On the south downs. I live close to the hills."

H: "What's so great about this?"

C: "I love the fresh air. And the views. You know? I love the vistas."

H: "You love the fresh air and the vistas."

C: "Yeah."

H: "The fresh air and the vistas. How do they make you feel?"

C: "Alive. Really good. I feel happy."

H: "So you feel happy."

C: "Yeah. Its nice."

H: "What else do you feel?"

C: "I feel happy and peaceful and calm."

H: "You feel happy and peaceful and calm."

C: "Yeah. Yeah, I do."

H: "Can you feel that same happy and peaceful and calm now?"

C: "Yeah, I can. It's nice."   (Their eyes are slightly glazed.)

H: "That's it." (Pause.)

H: "Where are you feeling happy and peaceful and calm?"

C: "Here, I think. It's here." (Signalling to chest)

H: "So you feel happy and peaceful and calm there."

C: "Yeah." (Eyes glazed more and deeper breathing)

H: "Can you make it more happy and peaceful and calm there?"

C: (Pauses...) "Yeah."

H: "And what is that like inside?"

C: (Long pause...) "Like a glowing light. Like a ball of light."

H: "Like a glowing ball of light. And if you make that bigger ... how nice is that?"

C: "That's really nice." (eyes begin to blink

more)

H: "And how are you doing that?"

C: (Pause...) "I don't know"

H: "That's right, you don't know. And you don't have to say anything, but I wonder if you realise that as you go deeper into hypnosis that your eyes have started to blink more..."

C: "Umm ..."

H: "and as your eyes start to blink more you can go deeper into hypnosis; but I don't want you to close those eyes just yet, not until you are reeeaally ready now to feel happy and peaceful and calm. And as you..."

(Client closes their eyes and breathes out deeply.)

H: "That's it. Really good."

And that's it. It really is as simple as that. In fact, it is often somewhat easier that that! This transcript included elements that are not mentioned in the basic process on page 23 and which I had not thought about using beforehand, like asking them to increase the size of the ball of light. However, I have left them in because they demonstrate how flexible this induction really can be.

On first reading, you might now think that the Leisure Induction seems too easy and straightforward, but I can honestly say that it has never failed me. Not once.

Before I move on to dissecting this particular transcript, have another read of it and note the places where I shift from a past tense to present-tense, or from an external focus to an internal one. You will be able to see how smoothly this can be done, as well as noting that at times you can be explicit about those shifts and at other times you can be more indirect.

**EXERCISE:**

Read back over the transcript before going any further.

Take note of any words or actions that surprised you.

As you read the commentary below, it may be worthwhile considering how you could have said or done anything differently.

If you have questions about the transcript that are not answered in the commentary, write them down as they come up. There's a good chance they will be answered as we progress.

GRAHAM OLD

# A Retrospective Commentary

Further transcripts and notes are provided throughout this book. Along the way, we will dig into the core principles at work and the skills demonstrated at each stage. However, before we get that far involved, let's proceed by looking at an overview of what has taken place in this first transcript.

There were seven stages, or movements, in this version of the induction and – if you haven't already done so – you might want to see if you can discover them for yourself before moving on.

As I emphasise the flexibility and adaptability of the Leisure Induction, it would be inconsistent to now provide you with scripts or solid structures to slavishly follow. Indeed, there was no strict structure in mind before this session took place, other than a basic guideline similar to that seen on p.19 above. However, it is possible to look at this transcript retrospectively and note the movements that took place and offer some thoughts on why it developed as it did.

## What?

You only need to begin by asking your client what they

enjoy doing. In Appendix A, I have provided a number of different ways of asking the same question, but you can simply just ask, *"what is your favourite leisure activity?"* This immediately gets them to think about good things and their mind goes off to find the activity - and part of them begins to re-experience it. Once they identify it, we have something to work with..

So in this example, I said:


Hypnotist: "Tell me what is your favourite leisure activity?"


Client: "I love walking on the hills. I love being outside in the fresh air."


H: "You love walking on the hills and being in the fresh air?"


C: "Yeah, it's great."


If, for whatever reason, you feel that you can not use the activity offered – perhaps it appears to have no element of 'trance' within it, or something makes it unhelpful to explore further – you simply carry on as you would in normal conversation, by asking, "What else?" However, it at all possible, you simple take what they say and feed it back.

## Where and When?

I then directed their mind to go to the place they enjoy so they would actually start experiencing it. A straightforward and natural way to do this is to put them *in the time & location* where they enjoyed it. I did it in this example like so:

H: "Where do you do this?"

C: "On the south downs. I live close to the hills."

H: "On the south downs."

C: "Yeah."

H: "When do you do this?"

C: "Weekends usually. When the mood takes me"

H: "Weekends, when the mood takes you..."

C: "Yeah."

This is an incredibly subtle way to get them to start experiencing their leisure activity. I prefer this approach to the more direct, "Now imagine yourself on the south downs". Partly, this is because it is unnecessary - they are already doing that! – but I also value the feeling of power that a client gets from being in the driving seat. As far as they are concerned, all I am doing at this stage in the journey is asking about the sights and sounds along the way.

The beauty of this approach is that you do not even need to have decided by this point if you are going to move into hypnosis. This is a very normal conversation so far, which could veer off into any number of directions. In fact, this is a common way for me to begin a therapy session, regardless of whether or not I will be using hypnosis.

## Why?

The reason anyone does a leisure activity is usually for enjoyment and/or their benefit. In fact, Stephen Brooks states that the reason people get hooked on leisure activities is because they are so often trance-inducing.

You may be surprised at the kinds of activities people take part in, to experience these enriching 'trances'. I remember working with a client who enjoyed long distance running and as soon as I asked the upcoming question he suddenly displayed a number of signs that he was going into hypnosis. It really surprised me. Similarly, I once worked with a man who enjoyed lifting heavy weights at the gym. I thought to myself, "working out is hardly a good way to get someone into hypnosis", but he told me afterwards that he felt great and that he actually had the sensation of sweat on his arms! The important thing to remember is that its each to their own. Sweaty arms doesn't do it for me, but it definitely did it for him.

Back to the induction - and I asked:

H: "What's so great about walking on the hills?"

C: "I love the fresh air. And the views. You know? I love the vistas."

There are a number of ways to ask the same question:

• "So, what is it you enjoy about walking on the hills?"

• "Why do you value that so much?"

• "How come?"

In fact, you don't even need to finish the question:

"And, what is it about walking on the hills...?"

The *Why* question is effective because, believe it or not, some people will never have thought about it and will need to access their previous experience slightly just to answer you. They may not have been explicitly aware that the reason they value walking in the countryside is because they like the feeling of freedom, or that what they get from swimming is that sense of floating free of any worries or stress.

When my client above said they, "love the fresh air. And the views", she actually took a deep breath in and appeared to be looking off into the distance as she answered. Noticing these sort of things is a real confidence boost, as you know someone is genuinely engaging with you and (importantly) enjoying themselves.

## How?

Next, I simply continued with the classic "5 Ws and 1H" questions, by asking, "How?". I know *what* it is that they like to do and I know *when* and *where* they do it. However, I wanted to further investigate what it was that they gained from the activity, as it is this that will cause them to re-live it.

So, I decided to ask them how their activity made them feel, by finding out what difference it makes to them.

In effect, what I was doing at this stage was exploring their answer to *Why* – by finding out *How* walking on the Hills gave them the benefit they said it did.

This was where I first really began to shift focus from the external, to the internal. As you will see in the Structural Variations in Appendix B, one way to proceed with these questions is to move through the senses until you get to Taste and Touch / Feelings, which then easily turns attention inwards. However, as I was taking a different approach, I used the Why and How questions to the same end.

H: "The fresh air and the vistas. How do they make you feel?"

C: "Alive. Really good. I feel happy."

H: "So you feel alive and happy."

C: "Yeah. Its nice."

Feeling alive and being happy is a very good thing! So I wanted to encourage it further. I did this in my response, which was just repeating what they had said to me. Yet, notice there is no question mark – I'm reiterating the fact that they *are* feeling their leisure activity in the here and now and reinforcing it with what *they say* it makes them feel. Its the same as saying, "At this very moment, you are feeling alive and happy", but it's less work for me and more control for the client. Don't be afraid to let go of the controls!

"Alive" and "happy" are good but I almost always ask, "What else?", because there are always more good feelings to come out of enjoyable experiences.

H: "What else do you feel?" (They are already in the moment, so I explore it further.)

C: "I feel happy and peaceful and calm."

H: "You feel happy and peaceful and calm."

C: "Yeah. Yeah, I do."

H: "Can you feel that same happy and peaceful and calm now?"

C: "Yeah, I can. Its nice." (Eyes slightly glazed.)

H: "That's it." (Said in a reassuring tone).

C: (No response)

Notice that the client responds with, "Yeah. Yeah, I do" and not, "Yeah, I did". This shows that she truly is experiencing those feelings again in the present moment.

I then checked-in with the client to confirm (to them, as much as to me) that they can access those feelings in the present, even though their demeanour has already left this beyond doubt. It was a way of drawing their attention to the here-and-now nature of their recollection.

Another useful tip is to use the Ericksonian sound-bite, "That's it". It doesn't require an answer from the client. Instead, it reassures and encourages them to keep feeling the way they do. It also tells them they are doing everything they should be.

## Explore

So the next step was to explore those feelings even further, cementing the new internal focus of their experience. In this example, I was explicit about asking them to identify where inside they are feeling them.

H: "Where are you feeling happy and peaceful and calm?"

C: "Here I think. Its here." (signalling to chest)

H: "So you feel happy and peaceful and calm there."

C: "Yeah." (eyes glazed more and deeper breathing)

I have already situated them in the present and confirmed that they are currently accessing their previous feelings. It is now as if we fully shift from the past to the present and let them see that the experience can carry on even now.

Once you are at this stage you can give yourself a pat on the back. You can be assured that your client is fully engaged with the process, as they can physically identify the feeling inside as a present reality. This will also tell you that you are moments away from them going "fully under", so to speak.

I wanted the client to be able to *increase* those positive feelings. I did that by very simply asking them to. It sounds incredibly easy. And it is!

H: "Can you make it *more* happy and peaceful and calm there?"

C: (Pauses) "Yeah."

You may feel uncomfortable asking them, "Can you ...?"

It can be a bit of a risk, because it's a closed question. That is, they will most likely answer "yes" or "no". So you might find it beneficial to be more indirect and permissive.

Perhaps you could say, "You might want to take your time to make it more happy and peaceful and calm there" or, "I wonder how quickly you will start to feel more happy and peaceful and calm there". At times, you may have preferences, depending on your style or approach. On this occasion, I can only say that – being lead by my client - it felt the most natural way to ask the question.

## Expand

This is really a continuation of the exploration stage. However, I want the client to build on their (now ongoing) experience and to extend those feelings in a tangible way. One way to do this is by finding out how they are experiencing the feelings internally and then play around with the sub-modalities.

(In some ways, we have something of a deepening spiral going on here. I started by asking what they get out of their activity and then explored that further by asking *how* they get that benefit. Now, having lead them to an internal focus, I ask what they are currently getting out of their activity – and then explore that further by asking how they are currently experiencing that.)

The purpose of my questioning at this stage was to drill down into the finer details of the client's feelings to deepen their current experience. My question was sufficiently vague that my client could have answered in any number of ways. For example, they could quite feasibly have just said, "It's nice" or "It's like a long massage." However, fortunately for me, they answered in such a way that I could easily satisfy my quirk for shifting sub-modalities.

We can think of our experiences as being filtered through our senses – sight, sound, touch, smell, and taste. These are sometimes referred to as *modalities*. However, within each modality there are fine details which we can call the *submodalities*. To find a submodality, it can help to think of *how* you see something, *how* you hear it and so on. For example, an image can be big or small, black & white or in colour; a sound can be loud or quiet, close or far away and so on.

On this occasion, I kept my language 'clean' and allowed the client to choose their own submodality. (At other times, I might choose a sub-modality that they have not used yet, just to expand and deepen their experience even further.) By doing this you'll see they experience at least 5 things:

1. They don't question, analyse or criticise the feeling

2. They actively explore the experience

3. They enjoy the feeling

4. They want to feel "it" even more

5. They go deeper into hypnosis very quickly as they conduct a 'transderivational search'

If you haven't come across this delightfully grandiose term before, a transderivational search (TDS) takes place when someone is presented with vague or ambiguous content, leading them to look inside their mind for the meaning and understanding. It's a very powerful tool in hypnosis, as it provides a natural way to redirect someone's focus inwardly.

Don't be surprised if your client is slower in responding to your questions at this point. Be confident that they are actually going deeper into hypnosis because of the questions you're asking. It's a very good sign.

Here's what I said next:

H: "And what is that like inside?"

C: (Long pause...) "Like a glowing light. Like a ball of light."

H: "Like a glowing ball of light. And if you make that bigger ... how nice is that?"

C: "That's really nice." (Eyes begin to blink more)

I simply asked her to imagine what it was like, fed her

response back and then asked her to explore it by making it bigger.

However, you don't have to ask her to make it bigger. In fact, you can use any sub-modality you want. The important thing is to increase the intensity of the sub-modality and use the language the client uses.

(I've always found that by increasing the sub-modality, they experience it more and this intensifies the feeling for them. Here's something you might want to try out: you can always ask them to make the submodality/feeling so big that they can step into it. Then you can ask them how that feels. This is a very powerful way of immersing them in the feeling and has always proved beneficial.)

If you look at the transcript above, you'll notice other places where I am leading the client to *Explore* and *Expand* their experience. For example:

> H: "Can you feel that same happy and peaceful and calm now?"

And:

> H: "That's right, you don't know. And you don't have to say anything, but I wonder if you realise that as you go deeper into hypnosis that your eyes have started to blink more..."

The terminology used is not really all that important. The important thing is to allow your client to slow down and internalise their experience and as they do so you can guide them to intensify that experience. Effectively, they have moved from remembering an experience to recreating and reliving it. They then increase that experience and – through exploratory questions like this – begin to own it for themselves, before fully entering into it.

It is this last step that we turn to now.

## Release

I have called this last step, 'Release'. The reason I've called it that is because I have been fortunate enough to experience this induction many times and I know that when I am at this stage, I am yearning to go even deeper into hypnosis. In fact, I want to be set free from the induction so that I can fully experience hypnosis! However, by holding back and allowing someone to wait, we can build anticipation and create a deeper sense of hypnosis.

Let's recap for a moment. You've got someone to remember an enjoyable state; you've got them to internalise their feelings and experience this state in the present tense; then you've got them to increase the intensity of the state so they are actually feeling it in the here and now... or maybe even experience being immersed in the feeling.

Then you ask a question that seems to contradict everything we've said and also engages the critical/analytical side of their brain. Nonetheless, even though it may not initially look like it, this helps them to search even deeper inside themselves and can be the tipping point into hypnosis. Simply put, you ask them a question that they don't know the answer to!

In this case, that question was:

H: "How are you doing that?"

C: (Pause.) "...I don't know"

Or:

H: "And how did you know to do that?"

C: (Pause.) "...I don't know"

There is a reason why this is so effective. As your client does not know the answer, they have to once again go even deeper inside themselves to find the answer, but they never can. Yet, they go inside with the nagging sense that there is a connection now between the behaviours they are demonstrating and going even deeper inside. Instead of confusing them or making them more critical and analytical, this round of questioning assists them to actually go deeper into hypnosis. It is as if their mind has become in awe of the experience.

I know that might sound strange, but it really does work. Not knowing something in this state of mind (a mind that feels safe and is enjoying the experience) is confusing, but it is an unusually pleasant confusion. It is as if they marvel at the power of the unknown, creating yet another inner search. This only serves to deepen the hypnosis further.

You then feed all of this back to them by repeating, "that's right, you don't know". What you have effectively created at this stage is an internal experiential loop. They have an experience, which you intensify, that they cannot fully make sense of. This all happens whilst the experience continues to expand and so on.

We discuss 'deepening' a little later, but you will have already seen how it is included seamlessly within the induction. At this stage, it is as if you bring their experience to a peak and then finally allow them to drop down into hypnosis.

That all may sound just too easy to be true. Yet, this induction really is as simple as asking someone how they like to relax and then exploring their answer to deeper and deeper levels until they talk themselves all the way into hypnosis!

**EXERCISE:**

Practice the Leisure Induction using the Basic Process as a guide, if necessary.

In fact, Practice every opportunity you get!

Your aim is to reach the point where it feels to you and to your practice-partner as if you are just having a normal conversation, not as if you are inflicting a technique on someone.

# Core Principles

We turn now to examine the core principles functioning within the Leisure Induction. As you learn these, be aware that you are also learning about some of the core principles often at work in any effective hypnotic interaction.

## Revivification

The first principle seen in the Leisure Induction is that of *Revivification*. To revivify means to restore to life, revive or reanimate.

In this context, revivification is more than simply recalling something, though that is often how it begins. Although we may start by simply asking someone about their favourite leisure activity, in reality we are getting them to recall a previous experience of trance and then to go on to relive it.

Part of the reason that we feed back what the client is saying is to situate them in their retelling of their experience. After all, we do not want them to simply say, "I like to play Golf." Instead, what we want for them is to undergo the experience of playing golf *in the here and now*. The answers they provide, following an internal search to answer our questions, flesh out the details and make their recollection more real.

Additionally, the feeding back of those answers also acts as something of an embedded command, as if you were saying, "...and do that now" to each answer that is given.

Each question that is asked invites your client to relive some small part of the answer. For example, if I were to ask you, "what did it feel like when you were scared watching that movie?" you would have to feel at least some of that fear again to be able to accurately answer the question.

This is an essential element in hypnotic revivification. In order to properly recall a previous experience of trance (or relaxation, or confidence, or unwinding, or hypnosis, or any state), the client has to begin to relive certain aspects of it. The more they are encouraged to do this - via different senses and in different modalities - the more likelihood there is that you will have a hypnotic revivification.

A very simple way to use revivification to your advantage – and a very acceptable way to begin this induction – is to start by asking about any previous experiences with hypnosis. This carries the wonderfully subtle presumption that they are about to enter into hypnosis again. Yet, it also implies the kind of things that the client should look out for, as well as the aspects of experience that they should prepare for as the conversation progresses.

In essence, the revivification at work within the Leisure

Induction is an example of utilisation, taking your clients experience with trance (or something like it) and employing it to assist you in leading them into hypnosis.

## Utilisation

Utilisation could just as easily be categorised as a core *skill* in the Leisure Induction. However, we are including it here as it is also a fundamental principle of Ericksonian hypnosis. In fact, Erickson considered one of his two original contributions to the field of psychotherapy to be his concept of utilisation, radically accepting and using whatever the client may bring, however difficult or troublesome it may seem at first glance.

No surprise then that Stephen Gilligan writes:

> 'Appreciating and utilizing the "realities" of the client [is] the basis for all hypnotic and therapeutic developments.'[3]

There is really no limit to how this can be applied. If your client comes in angry, use that anger. If they are tired, utilise their tiredness. If they complain of a neck-ache part way through your session, use that neck-ache to your (and their) advantage.

My clinic is based within a Complementary Health Centre and it is not unusual to hear a telephone ringing

---

3  Stephen G. Gilligan (1987). *Therapeutic Trances*. New York: Routledge. p.98.

from another office, or even to hear a door opening in the distance. When this happens, I often employ these potential distractions in making statements like:

> "And you may find that as your mind opens to new possibilities, you can allow the door to gently close on that past. The past is called the 'passed' for good reason. And once we learn a lesson, we don't need to keep going back..."

Or:

> "And part of you may continue to be aware of sounds around you, in the back of your mind, reminding you what a natural every day experience this is..."

As stated above, the very nature of this induction is an exercise in discovering and utilising your client's previous experiences.

A simple way to explain utilisation, is just to say, *use whatever your client gives you*. After all, why go through the trouble of forcing your ideas and experiences into someone else's mind, when you can simply use theirs?

When they give you a verbal response, feed it back to them. As said, this can function as an embedded command, but is more than that. It is also a reassurance and an encouragement. Importantly, it functions as an acceptance of your client's experience. Thus, it assists rapport-building and reinforces the level of connection that you have with your client.

Additionally, when you receive a non-verbal response – the minimal cues spoken of below – you can utilise this also. Again, this reassures the client that something is happening, but has the added effect of inviting them to go 'inside' to investigate.

This may be why Bandler and Grinder described this approach as the easiest induction there is. Essentially, you ask someone to inform you how they went into trance before and then feed-back whatever they tell or show you. It is as if they hand you their own customised script and you simply read it back to them!

(To really get the best out of this book – and to ensure that its contents become something that you successfully put into practice – I would suggest reading that last paragraph again.)

## Nominalisations

Finally, it is worth mentioning nominalisations, as they can play an important role in the client's expanding experience (in other words, the "deepener") and are apt to be utilised.

Korzybski noted back in the 1930s that people often talked about processes e.g. thinking happily, wondering curiously, experiencing depressive feelings, as if they were static nouns – happiness, curiosity, depression, etc. In some situations, this can be unhelpful.

For example, although nominalisations might be thought to clarify and stream-line communication, they can lead to confusion and presumption and can therefore cause miscommunication. Some people make the mistake of presuming that they know what a client means when they use words like 'stress', 'depression' or even 'happiness'. Yet, there is no guarantee that someone is using a word in the same way you or I would to express their experience of the world.

Additionally, in a therapeutic context, when clients are over-focused on their own nominalisations it can create a sense of 'stuckness', or being locked in their current condition. After all, they have taken a fluid experiential process – feeling stress, or being overwhelmed with depressive thoughts and feelings – and expressed it as a concrete and rigid noun.

Nevertheless, for our current purposes, it is worth remembering that a nominalisation is yet another thing that can be utilised. In fact, nominalisations can be extremely useful in the right hands as they provide us with the means to communicate complex experiences in simple and non-specific ways.

For example, when using the Leisure Induction, you will frequently come across words like "freedom", "happiness", "peace", "escape" and so on. Yet, there is no such thing as "freedom" - it is a noun description of the condition or experience of being free. We can therefore use this in two ways.

Firstly, we can choose to ask questions to unpack a nominalisation, transforming it from a static description to a living experience. This can be seen in the transcript in the next section, where you'll also see the principles of revivification and utilisation being employed:

Hypnotist: "So, what do you enjoy doing...?"

Client: "Swimming. I'd swim all day long if I could."

H: "All day long."

C: "Yeah. I love it."

H: "What is it that you love about swimming?"

C: "Oh, so much! The freedom. Time to myself, to escape into my own little world..."

As already stated, 'Freedom' is a clear nominalisation, suitable for further unpacking. I could have asked what that freedom looks like, or what it feels like. That would have lead the client to consider and describe exactly what it was like when they 'escaped'.

The second way we can utilise nominalisations is by doing all of this in reverse. Once the client has begun to re-experience their previous trance, we now know that the simple phrase 'freedom' sums-up and evokes an experience that they find enjoyable. So, I don't need to struggle to come up with words to describe or elicit this experience for them.

In the following transcript, you will notice that I use the client's nomalisations both to sum-up and to anchor the state that I want them to re-experience. This means that we can be fairly content-free with our language and keep our suggestions clean. Unless I choose to unpack and utilise a nominalisation, I don't even need to know what a client means by 'freedom', or 'peace'. All I need to know is that I can use that word to lead them to recall – and ultimately to relive - an experience.

(If you are unsure on the nature of nominalisations, there is a whole host of them provided in Appendix C. However, the classic test for determining whether or not something is a nominalisation is to ask the question, "Could I put this in a wheelbarrow?" If the answer is "No", then you may well be dealing with a nominalisation.)

**EXERCISE:**

Ask a friend or family member to share a happy memory with you.

Using what you have learned so far, ask questions that will enable them to recollect more clearly. Afterwards, ask them for feedback on the process.

Repeat this exercise for someone else, but ask for feedback *during* the recollections, by asking the occasional question like, "What's it like now for you to recall that?" and "Can you get a sense of that now, as you remember it?"

GRAHAM OLD

# The Principles In Practice

We will provide another transcript here of the Leisure Induction in practice. You might choose to follow along and note the principles of revivification and utilisation, as well as noting the use of nominalisations.

There is only minor commentary following this transcript, as you will have a better idea by now of what is taking place.

Hypnotist: "So, what do you enjoy doing in your free time?"

Client: "Swimming. I'd swim all day long if I could."

H: "All day long."

C: "Yeah. I love it."

H: "What is it that you love about swimming?"

C: "Oh, so much! The freedom. Time to myself, to escape into my own little world..."

H: "Freedom. What is that like?"

C: "Oh, it's just time for me to leave everything else behind – work, *Him*, the kids – and just drift off."

H: "Drift off."

C: "Yeah, physically and mentally."

H: "So, when do you get to do this?"

C: "Well, not as often as I would like, but I try to get there at least once a week. Maybe after work."

H: "So, maybe once a week, after work, you go there and as you go there, you just drift off."

C: "Yeah"

# MASTERING THE LEISURE INDUCTION

H: "Leaving everything else behind"

C: (Smiles) "Yeah."

H: "And what is that like when you drift off?"

C: "Nice."

H: "And where do you get to do this?"

C: "Oh, just at the Sports Centre, in town."

H: "So, once a week, maybe after work, you're at the Sports Centre in town and as you're there you escape into your own little world."

C: "Yeah. It's Heaven." (Smiles a slow and gentle smile, matched with changes to their breathing.)

H: "And it looks like you're escaping there a bit now." (Smiles)

C: "I am!" (Laughs)

H: "Did you realise that your breathing has changed?"

C: "I hadn't. But I do now."

H: "And as you escape, leaving everything else behind, tell me, how does *that* feel now?

C: "It feels nice. Peaceful." (Blinking reflex has slowed down.)

H: "Peaceful."

C: "Yeah, you know, just drifting, nothing else going on."

H: "I know. Physically and mentally."

C: (Smiles) "Yeah".

H: "And tell me this then, as there is nothing else going on, what *is* going on with your eyelids."

C: (Blink) "I don't know."

H: "No. Did you know that your eyes would do that?"

C: "No."

H: "You didn't, did you?"

C: "No."

H: "And yet, here we are. Freedom to leave everything thing else behind. Just drifting..."

C: "Hmmhmmm..."

H: "And I really don't want you to close those eyes until you find yourself escaping, leaving everything else behind... right now."

C: (Deep breath)

H: "That's right..."

C: (Closes eyes)

H: "That's it. Into your own little world."

This was an interesting example of the Leisure Induction in practice. Initially, I felt that the client was not really engaging. I thought that I was using all of the right questions, but it seemed like it was going to be a struggle to lead the client inside. Then, it just happened!

In fact, when I directed the clients' attention to their eyes, what I was interested in was their fixed gaze. I had fully expected them to stay open in that condition for the remainder of the session (as can be fairly common with this induction). Yet, when they became aware that they were responding in ways that they had not intended to, it was as if their eyes instantly became heavy and they closed them within a few more blinks.

It is worth noting that if I had been reading a script, or been over-focused on a technique, I may have missed what was taking place in front of me.

**EXERCISE:**

Practice the Leisure Induction with a friend.

Decide beforehand if you are going to do so explicitly and directly (e.g. "Now, I would like you to close your eyes and begin to relive that memory"), or discreetly and indirectly.

Aim to stick with this decision if possible, for the purposes of practicing the induction. Later on, such pre-decisions will be irrelevant, as flexibility reigns supreme.

Begin to pay more attention to your use of the Core Principles and notice what effect this has on your friend.

GRAHAM OLD

# Core Skills

## Observation

If I could imprint only two words on the minds of every newly qualified Hypnotherapist, those two words would be 'Observation' and 'Utilisation'. When I first began my career in hypnosis, I trained with two of the giants in contemporary Hypnosis, Jonathan Chase and Stephen Brooks. From Chase, I learned the importance of my own personal presence and belief in myself and the art and power of hypnosis. From Brooks, I learned about the importance of Observation and Utilisation. From beginning to end, through stories, case-studies and demonstrations, Brooks emphasised  and demonstrated their importance. I, for one, am glad he did.

It may seem strange for training in a practical skill to focus on such conceptual matters. However, the focus that Brooks placed on Observation and Utilisation was enough to completely change my approach and redirect my therapeutic practice.

That may seem like a grand claim for what is essentially quite a simple point, yet it remains true. This fresh focus challenged my ideas about what it is that I am seeking to do in therapy, as well as how I would proceed to do it.

In fact, I now tell my own students that there is nothing I have to teach them that is more important than this suggestion from Freud:

> 'Suspend judgement and give impartial attention to everything there is to observe.'[4]

We have stated above that Utilisation is one of the core principles at work in the Leisure Induction. Yet, you have to first notice something before you can make use of it!

Observation is a particularly important skill when it comes to this induction, as you need to be ready to feed back what the client does, not just what they say. What you will be looking for are the small physical changes that tell you your client is responding. From an Ericksonian perspective, these observable signs are often referred to as "minimal cues" of trance. Whether or not that is an accurate description is well beyond the scope of this book to argue. However, what they do seem to reveal is when the subject is having an internal experience that matches their external descriptions – that is, they are no longer just recalling a previous experience; they are effectively re-living it.

You may be surprised at how obvious some of these signs are. You may even be surprised that you didn't notice them before. Regardless, keep your eyes open and you will be unlikely to miss them again.

The great thing about these signs is that they can be a highly reliable barometer of how someone is responding

---

4 Freud, S. (1909). Analysis of a phobia in a five-year old boy. *Standard Edition*, 10, 3-152. London: Hogarth Press, 1955.

internally. So, they can increase your confidence that things are proceeding as hoped, as well as informing your client that they are responding appropriately.

Here are some of the signs you will want to look out for. Maybe just one, or maybe all. But once you see them you can be confident that you have an effective revivification:

- Glazed eyes

- Pupils dilating

- Deeper breathing

- Flushed cheeks

- Flattening of the facial muscles

- Changes in skin colour

- Eye watering

- Twitching hands, arms or legs

- Slow response and speech

- Fixed gaze

- Non-responsiveness

- Frozenness / full body catalepsy

- Changes in blink rate

- Slowing of the swallow reflex

Once you see these, you can utilise them and feed them back to go even 'deeper', but more on that later.

## Genuine Listening

We come now to what is perhaps the most conspicuous aspect of the Leisure Induction. Yet, as unnatural as it may at first appear, it plays a vital role.

We have highlighted in a number of places the importance of feeding back what your client says to you. There are a number of reasons for this, which we have previously alluded to and will say more about below. The thing to take on board at this point is that this is both more and less than the common therapeutic practice of Active or Reflective Listening.

We do not simply let the client speak and then paraphrase back what they have said. Instead, we repeat it back *exactly as they said it*. As Judy Rees puts it, this is more "parrot-phrasing" than paraphrasing.

Using the same vocabulary as someone else is a well-established way to build rapport and trust, as well as expressing interest and respect. Richard Wiseman quotes a study from the University of Nijmegen in which a waitress increased her tips by 70 per cent simply by repeating the customer's order back to them, rather than merely saying "okay" or "coming right up".[5]

---

5 Wiseman, Richard (2009). *59 Seconds: Think A Little, Change A Lot*. Oxford: Macmillan. pp.162-163.

Feeding back in this way indicates that you are really listening, rather than simply waiting for your turn to speak. Significantly, by repeating their words to them, what the client hears is that you want to hear more of what they have to say.

By repeating what they have actually said, rather than what you think they really meant, you also underline to the speaker what they are saying, giving them the opportunity to correct or expand their statements.

It is common for students to wonder if this will be too obvious, or if it will sound insincere. However, in my experience, it can often have the opposite effect. Instead of working out how to cleverly paraphrase your client's words, you are free to *actually listen to what they are really saying*. When you think of listening as a form of observation, you can perhaps begin to see how your client will experience your interaction with them as one of genuine interest.

We have said enough about the way that your feedback – either of what is said, or of the minimal cues your client is showing – encourages people to go inside to check the veracity of what you, or they, have said. However, it might be beneficial to say a little more about how this provides the opportunity for embedded commands.

In the transcript below, we see this example:

H: "So, *you're comfortable*, slowing down, getting *in that zone*... And what more is there to getting lost in the moment? What does that feel like?"

C: "It's just peaceful. A time to escape."

H: "And you *value that peaceful*, that '*time to escape*'... [Begin to match their breathing, speaking on the exhale]. What else is there that *feels good* about that slowing down... getting in that zone... just peaceful... time to escape?"

The italicised words are there to demonstrate just how easily and naturally the words that we feed back can function as embedded commands.

Not only are we increasing the clients revivification, redirecting their focus inward or affirming what they have said, but we are feeding back suggestions that they have already told us will enable them to experience trance.

## Pacing, Leading & Contingent Suggestions

We now turn to a language pattern that experienced hypnotists may employ throughout their speech, but which particularly features in the Leisure  Induction – pacing current experience and contingent suggestions.

Although this skill is used throughout the induction, it serves different purposes at different points. At the earliest stages, it increases the sense of flow and process, whilst later on it helps with pacing and leading and deepening their experience.

When our clients are providing information on the experience they are recalling, if we do nothing more than repeat back their words to them it can cause the induction to feel staggered and even disconnected. So, we use linking language to create smooth transitions, increasing the feeling of a flowing process.

> H: "So, you're comfortable, slowing down, getting in that zone... And what more is there to getting lost in the moment?"

This implicitly reminds the client that all of these events are not unconnected, but are part of a process that lead them in to trance. Moreover, it places them in that process much more easily than if we were simply reading out a bullet-point list of each aspect of their recollection.

The extent of the linking used in the example above is not completely conveyed in written form. The rhythm of what was said was just as important as the content to express the smooth transitions from one thing to the next. This is why we have not simply labeled this section "Use Conjunctions". In reality, your language could be very static, but the delivery (including your body language whilst speaking) can still convey the sense of a progressive flow.

However, if you choose, you can make the linkage explicit, even including it in your questions:

> Client: "I like laying in my hammock."

Hypnotist: "Laying in your hammock. And what is it that you like about laying in your hammock?"

C: "Um... I can just let go and be." (Smiles)

H: "So, as you're laying in your hammock you can just let go and be. And then what?"

Asking "and then what" is effectively the same as asking "What else", but it feeds into the feeling of process and keeps it going.

When such language is used throughout the induction, it begins to feel completely natural to both the hypnotist and the client. One benefit of this is that the later introduction of pacing and leading language does not appear obtrusive.

Observant readers may have already realised that this skill is yet another example of utilisation. The idea is to build a link between what the client is currently experiencing (pacing) and what you would like them to do next (leading). To use this language pattern skilfully, you can also employ it as a 'Yes set', a patterned response of accepting what you are saying. Establishing an agreeable frame of mind in this way enhances rapport whilst also planting a receptiveness to continue to respond in an affirmative manner.

An example from the next section demonstrates this perfectly:

H: "So, as you're laying in your hammock, you can just let go and be. And your body sinks into it as your tension begins to float away...And as you leave the worries of the day behind, you can allow yourself to drift deeper into that bliss now."

You will note that this suggestion incorporates feedback, nominalisations, a Yes Set and a contingent suggestion. The suggestion at the end hitch-hikes the response of 'drift[ing] deeper into that bliss' onto their ongoing experience.

As can be seen in the next section, when contingent suggestions are used as a deepening technique, the hypnotist observes the client's non-verbal responses (their 'minimal cues') and includes them within the suggestions. For example, our very first transcript included this:

H: "I wonder if you realise that as you go deeper into hypnosis that your eyes have started to blink more..."

C: "Umm..."

H: "and as your eyes start to blink more you can go deeper into hypnosis, but I don't want you to close those eyes just yet, not until you are reeeaally ready now to feel happy and peaceful and calm. And as you..."

(Client closes their eyes and breathes out deeply.)

There is even a contingent suggestion used just at the end, yet worded as a negative. Ordinarily, contingent suggestions are as simple as saying, "As you X, then you can Y". However, as seen here, words such as "until" can also be used when prefixed by a negative, effectively saying: "don't do Y, until you X."

**EXERCISE:**

Practice Listening with a friend or family member. Do not do this as a technique, but to actually hear what they are saying to you.

Get a sense for what it feels like to pay attention to someone. When you are at this point, begin to feed-back, but only so that the person talking to you knows that they are being listened to.

Next, practice listening with someone else. This time, practice feeding back as a way to reassure someone that you are listening and to affirm them in what they are saying.

Only at this stage are you now ready to use feedback as a means to ascertain more information. Practice doing this is such a way that the person speaking feels like you are genuinely interested (not as an implied criticism that they have not given you enough information).

Finally, begin to notice any signs that your speaker is 'going inside' to access information. Feed this back as appropriate.

GRAHAM OLD

# The Skills On Display

Hypnotist: "Tell me about a time when you found yourself doing something you were totally engrossed in. Something you enjoyed, something you did where you are relaxed and yet totally absorbed. You know, where you maybe lose track of time for a while and your level of awareness seems to change?"

Client: "Yeah, sure. I get that whenever I paint."

H: "Ah, you paint. And what is it that you enjoy about painting?"

C: "I don't know. The colours. The creativity. It feels a bit like everything slows down while I kinda get in this creative zone."

H: "Everything slows down. It's funny that you

said you don't know what you enjoy about it, because clearly on one level you do.”

C: "Yeah."

H: “You enjoy slowing down in that zone.”

C: "Yeah. Definitely."

H: “Is this something you do on your own or with others?”

C: “On my own. I've always gotta be on my own?”

H: “Because...”

C: “It's just part of the whole peace and quiet thing. I can focus then and just get, like, lost in the moment.”

H: “Hmmm... Lost in the moment. What a great phrase.”

C: "Yeah." (Smiles)

H: "So, what is that like, that 'lost in the moment'?"

C: "It's like..."

H: "Wait, hold that thought. Before you go there, are you painting inside or outside?"

C: "Ah, inside. But by a window. So, I'm painting outside scenes, but I'm in the comfort of the inside." (Laughs)

H: "Well, comfort's important." (Both laugh)

H: "So, you're comfortable, slowing down, getting in that zone... And what more is there to getting lost in the moment? What does that feel like?"

C: "It's just peaceful. A time to escape."

H: "And you value that peaceful, that 'time to

escape'... [Begins to match their breathing, speaking on the exhale] What else is there that feels good about that slowing down... getting in that zone... just peaceful... time to escape?"

C: (Pauses, looking off to the left corner of the ceiling)

H: (Nods slowly, as if to affirm their 'lost in thought' experience)

H: "You look like you're escaping now!"

C: "Yeah." (Laughs) "I'm just thinking about slowing down and how that feels."

H: "And have you noticed the changes in your breathing yet... slowing down?"

C: "I hadn't, but, yeah." (Laughs) "That's weird."

H: "How did you know... that slowing down... changing your breathing... is the first part of going into trance?"

C: "I don't know."

H "That's right. You really don't know, do you? You're only just beginning to learn the things that you know, that you didn't know that you know. And I wonder, do you find it easier to increase that 'peaceful, slowing down', as you recall painting and all of the feelings associated with it, or if you simply escape right into that zone that painting takes you to now?"

C: (Client does not answer, but stares off into space)

H: "That's right. Muscles relaxing. Body slowing down. And as your body slows down, your mind can escape... into that zone... Peaceful."

C: (Client's breathing has slowed dramatically, with a couple of very deep exhalations. Their gaze had frozen off in the distance, but now their eyelids appear to blink rapidly.)

H: (Said with a slight shift of the head, as if speaking towards the corner of the room where the client got 'lost in thought'...) "That's it."

H: "And as your eyes begin to blink more, you can find yourself going deeper into that. But I don't want you to close your eyes... until you are ready to fully return to that place... See what you see. Hear what you hear. Feel what you feel. Enjoying that, slowing down... getting in that zone... just peaceful..."

C: (Clients eyes close)

H: "That's it... Time to escape..."

**EXERCISE:**

As you continue to practice the Leisure Induction, you can increase your use of linking language. As you do so, focus on re-creating a fluid experience for your practice-partner.

What you are trying to do is to re-create that experience *with* them, to enable you to then intensify it and eventually lead it in new and potentially deeper directions.

A common approach is to start with three pacing statements, followed by one leading suggestion. For example: "And as you sit there (P), your eyes blinking (P) and your breathing slow (P), you can begin to wonder just how much of that 'calm peace' you can continue to feel now (L)."

The next step, for practice purposes, is to repeat the entire process each time giving fewer paces and more leads (3 paces to 1 lead, 3 paces to 2 leads, 2 paces to 3 leads and 1 pace to 3 leads).

GRAHAM OLD

# Going Deeper

We move now to an area that we are often asked about, but which you will actually have already mastered if you have taken on board the skills and principles discussed so far – the "deepener".

Traditionally, some people think of a hypnotic experience as consisting of:

- Pre-talk

- Induction

- Deepener

- Therapy and/or phenomena

- Wake-up

However, if you have read *The Anatomy of Inductions* then you will know that we think of the induction as an essential part of a fluid therapeutic process, so are less inclined to think in this kind of way. Additionally, with the Leisure Induction, the dynamic nature of the process is accentuated, leaving less use for such static models.

From the moment you begin to re-direct your client's

focus inward, you are intensifying their experience, i.e. 'deepening' them. In other words, the deepening that takes place is  not a one-time event, but a continuation and enhancement of the entire experience.

That said, there are a number of tools to use, demonstrated both in the example below and in the initial and subsequent transcripts, which can assist the intensification of your client's inner absorption. In reality, these options will feel more integrated than the following classifications would imply.

## Changing Sub-modalities

As seen in our first transcript, inviting your client to adjust their sub-modalities is a useful way of focusing, exploring and thus deepening their internal reality.

## Feed back Minimal Cues

When it comes to minimal cues, the hypnotist's role is to reflect them back as they occur, acting as a kind of bio-feedback machine. This creates a hypnotic loop, clearly seen in the example below, where contingent suggestions are employed to link one response to the next.

## Nominalisations

As you reach the stage where you are intending to intensify your client's internal response, you can employ your own nominalisations as much as theirs. The key here is to use content-free words that the client will not reject, because they supply their own meaning (often doing so following a TDS).

## Contingent Suggestions

As discussed above, contingent suggestions can be used to pace your client's current experience and then add suggestions for an intensification of that same experience.

The following transcript demonstrates well how the deepening part of the Leisure Induction is in fact simply a continuation of the entire process. You will see how the elements above are used from the very beginning, yet take on an added role as the client's focus turns inward and the hypnotist leads them to deepen and enhance that internal experience.

**EXERCISE:**

With a partner, practice the Leisure Induction, including the elements of deepening. However, practice with an attitude that your aim is for them to have a rich and enjoyable experience, not for you to perform well.

Ask for feedback from them afterwards. Pay particular attention to times when they suggest their recollections were especially 'real'. Don't be surprised if this fluctuates throughout the induction.

# Deepening In Action

Hypnotist: "I'd be interested in hearing what you like to do to relax."

Client: "Well, in an ideal world, when the Sun is out, I like laying in my hammock."

H: "Laying in your hammock."

C: "Yeah."

H: "Where is this hammock?"

C: "In my back garden. I'm an optimist!" (Laughs)

H: "And what is it that you like about laying in your hammock?"

93

C: "Um... I can just let go and be." (Smiles)

H: "So, as you're laying in your hammock you can just let go and be. And then what?"

C: "Well, I normally feel my body just kinda...sink into it."

H: "And then?"

C: "It's like when my body sinks into the hammock any of the work-stuff playing on my mind just floats away."

H: "The work stuff just floats away."

C: "Yeah, all the stress and tension just starts to melt away... It's bliss." (Smiles)

H: "And how is that bliss?"

C: "I... it's just like there's nothing else going on. Nothing else to worry about. I can just relax."

H: "There's nothing else going on. Nothing else to worry about."

C: "Mmmm."

H: "So, as you're laying in your hammock, you can just let go and be. And your body sinks into it as your tension begins to melt away...And as you leave the worries of the day behind, you can allow yourself to drift deeper into that bliss now."

C: (Takes a deep breath and breathes out slowly)

H: "And were you aware of those changes in your breathing?"

C: "No, well, yeah."

H: "And as the stress and tension starts to float away and your breathing slows down, as you drift deeper in that bliss, tell me what that bliss is like inside."

C: "It's still, like...peace and quiet." [Has begun to blink rapidly]

H: "And as you enjoy that peace and quiet inside, your eyes may begin to blink more, and as your eyes begin to blink more you can drift deeper into that bliss."

C: (Head drops down and comes up again, as if trying not to fall asleep)

H: "And as you get yourself even more comfortable, enjoying that peace and quiet, you may already be aware of the tendency for your eyes to want to close. But I don't want you to allow them to close until you are ready to drop all the way into trance."

C: (Head nods slowly)

H: "And as your breathing continues to slow down..."

# MASTERING THE LEISURE INDUCTION

C: (Eyes close)

H: "...as your eyes close, I wonder if you will drift fully into that bliss before or after your head comfortably drops down and your chin rests on your chest."

"And, having left the worries of the day behind, just letting go, you may be curious about all of the learnings that you can discover as you continue to drift down."

C: (Head falls forward and chin rests on chest-bone)

H: "That's it."

"And isn't it interesting how easy you can find it to return to this place? Did you know you could return to bliss as easily as this?"

C: "No."

H: "You didn't did you? And still that part of you that is continuing to learn from this discovery, knew deep down how easily you could access that peace and quiet, this bliss..."

**EXERCISE:**

Continue to practice the Induction, paying attention to the use of nominalisations in 'deepening' the experience.

As you re-read the transcript above, notice how nominalisations can work in conjunction with pacing and leading. For example:

"And, having left the worries of the day behind, just letting go, you may be curious about all of the learnings that you can discover as you continue to drift down."

However, you can employ even more nominalisations as the deepening intensifies:

"You have already learned how you can experience this peace and serenity by understanding how easy it is for you to enjoy this discovery. And the learnings and fulfilment you continue to explore..."

The good news is that you do not have to be *overly* concerned with making sense, as your client will provide their own interpretation, following an internal search for meaning.

GRAHAM OLD

# Trouble-Shooting And FAQ

## Aren't you just using NLP?

We have been asked a few times if we are merely teaching Neuro-Linguistic Programming, usually by people surprised at how simple and effective this is. However, the fact is, we do not primarily teach NLP and do not particularly consider ourselves to be NLPers.

Nevertheless, in those places where NLP usefully summarises certain hypnotic principles and practices, it can be helpful to pass them on. This is the reason that we may occasionally use phrases like, 'Transderivational Search' and so on. However, our aim is always to teach the deeper principles at work, rather than simply the quick and handy way they were summarised.

## Are they genuine transcripts you have included?

It may be difficult to believe that such a simple induction could be so powerful, but, yes – these are all genuine transcripts.

We may have edited out a paragraph or two, but that is simply for the sake of space, or to avoid too much repetition. Nothing significant has been removed. In fact, the reason we used the initial transcript that we did was to show the level of flexibility and freedom that you have with this induction. Not everyone encounters balls of light, but when it happens, you just utilise it and carry on!

## I sound like a robotic Parrot when I feed back

This was partially addressed in the section on Listening, but it is worth exploring this further. If *all* you do is repeat back what is said to you – whether it is paraphrased or not – then you may well sound like a parrot. The idea is to genuinely listen and *then* feed-back, not merely restate what they have just said.

Before I give an example of what this may look like, it is worth bearing in mind that we are only feeding back, on average, the last 2 words said. So, it would sound nothing like this poor stereotype of a Counselling session:

Client: "I just feel so alone and depressed."

Therapist: "So, you are feeling depressed and as if you have to face this on your own?"

You would more likely sound like this:

"Alone and depressed."

However, if you paid particular attention to the transcripts contained in this book, then you may have noticed that even though you are repeating back what is said, you can still do so creatively. The following example demonstrates this well:

Client: "I like the feeling that I'm floating."

Hypnotist: "<u>Floating</u>."

C: "Yeah."

H: "Okay..."

C: "Just dropping everything and floating off on my own."

H: "And what is that about?"

C: "I don't know. Maybe, the ease of it?"

H: "And what do you value about that <u>ease</u>?"

C: "The lack of expectation."

H: "Mhmm"

C: "And, you know, just completely stress-free"

H: "So, it's the <u>lack of expectation</u>..."

C: "Yeah."

H: "<u>Completely stress-free</u>"

C: "Yeah, definitely."

H: "And what is *that* like? That <u>dropping everything and floating off on your own</u>?"

So, as you can see, even if all you are doing is feeding back, you can mix your responses round a little, begin or end the sentence with feedback, delay feedback, feedback partially and link responses together.

However, my experience has consistently been that if you focus more on genuinely listening and worry less about your technique, or what your client may or may not be thinking, it will invariably be welcomed.

## The Leisure activity they chose was not a good one

I would say, if at all possible, go with the answer your client gives you. Even if all it does is allow you to ask a few questions before you move on to a more suitable answer, you do not want to give the impression that your client somehow gave you the 'wrong' answer. However, on the whole, if they choose a leisure activity that they find valuable it will be because they experience it in enriching and entrancing ways.

Nevertheless, on occasion you will find that you just do not know how to utilise the answer they have given you. In that case, you simply proceed just as you would in a normal conversation - "And what else do you like to do?"

## What do I do if my client doesn't really react to their recollection?

It will happen that, at times, some people appear to keep a safe distance from anything resembling trance, whilst they tell you about their experiences. This can happen for a number of reasons. Sometimes, they intentionally resist getting too involved in their retelling, because they are trying hard to have a normal conversation. Other times, they may feel uneasy because they cannot make sense of what is happening to them, or they may feel nervous or scared about hypnosis. This can be particularly so if they sense that you are attempting to hypnotise them covertly.

Thankfully, neither of these reasons are insurmountable and there are a number of straightforward tactics you can employ to overcome this problem.

Firstly, you could simply ask them about something else they like to do. It could be that the initial leisure pursuit they opted for was not the most appropriate one they could have chosen. See above for more on this. However, even if the activity chosen was less than perfect, it can still have a fractionating effect to move through a number of different choices one after another.

(In hypnosis terms, Fractionation refers to the practice of repeatedly taking someone into and out of hypnosis. The idea is that, usually, the more that someone goes in and out of trance, the deeper they descend as they go back in.)

Secondly, before moving on to a different activity, it can be useful to briefly explain the phenomenon of natural 'trance'. You might describe the experiences that are common every day occurrences of something resembling hypnosis, whether that's daydreaming, 'highway hypnosis' whilst driving, being 'mesmerised' by a log-fire, or listening to music. That way, when you move on to the next leisure pursuit to discuss, you have already seeded the idea that this experience is linked to hypnosis.

Another option, for clients who seem to avoid re-living their experience in the here and now is to go direct. You can simply say something like, "Okay, well I would like you to now imagine that you are lying in your hammock right now. Tell me what it feels like as you sink into it and the worries of the day melt away."

It can be helpful to incorporate elements of the 'fake induction'[6] if this is a route you choose to go down.

---

6  See, for example, Graham Old. *The Fake Induction.*

## They appear to go into hypnosis, but never very deeply

This is a similar issue to that above. So, as well as the advice listed there, another option is to consider a kind of pattern-interrupt. For example, they may be re-telling their experience and dabbling around the edge of hypnosis when you abruptly say, "Okay, well, I'd like you to close your eyes now and become aware of your eyelids."

In our experience, the resultant induction (in this case, The Elman Induction) often seems to create a deeper absorption with its own unique qualities. In fact, even if you never face the issue of shallow responses, this is worth trying out for yourself.

## What do you do if someone becomes more animated by the discussion?

This is something that you might encounter when you first begin using the induction. So far, whenever I have come across someone who describes this 'problem', the issue is that they are forgetting to feed back the answers they are getting.

However, it is not really a problem at all. In fact, it often demonstrates that your client is invested in the activity they are describing, making it an apt choice. Simply remember to pause and feed back and speak at the pace that *you* wish to go. It is difficult for them to steam ahead if you keep interrupting them to calmly

---

http://www.howtodoinductions.com/inductions/fake.

repeat what they have just said.

## If you want someone to experience the result of their Leisure Activity in the here and now, why describe it as a past-tense experience at all?

This is a good question. It is true that we want to get from a recollection to a revivification. So, we could avoid the past-tense altogether. In fact, one of the Structural Variations in Appendix B takes this approach.

However, I have found that if I want someone to re-experience the effect of taking part in a leisure activity, it helps to employ an actual occurrence of that activity. That is, I do not want them to merely discuss the theoretical benefits of playing Golf; I want them to actually experience them. The most effective way to do this is by exploring a time when that has  happened in reality. This then gives them the details of the experience for them to report back to me, as well as letting them know what to expect as we go deeper into the process.

## How do you know what to feed back?

Having just mentioned feedback, it is worth remembering that you do not want to come across as someone who is simply repeating every single thing they say, not actually listening or interested in what they are saying. So, it can be tricky at first to know exactly what to feed back and what to utilise in other ways.

A helpful reminder is to keep in mind the embedded command function of some of this repetition. So, if I think repeating a word or two fulfils that function then I will almost always do so.

I also find it helpful to pick out the 'trancey' words that my clients use and feed them back. Words like relax, freedom, float, bliss, ease, dream and so on can be useful nominalisations to feed back.

At other times, I might want to unpack a nominalisation, if I feel that doing so will provide valuable information for me to use. For example, they may say that they like fishing because it "restores my soul". I may want to find out what the essence of this is for them, so that I can unpack the experience of "restoring their soul". To do this I might ask, "And what does 'it restores my soul' feel like?" and I may get the response "magical". I have now encouraged them to explore the experience at greater depth, got 2 nominalisations to use and come up with the word to feed back as an embedded command: magical. So I say, "you feel magical".

## Why do you sometimes seem to take someone into hypnosis and then bring them out again?

In reality, this happens whether we try to do it or not. At times, to answer a question, a client will need to go inside. Yet, the next thing they think about may again be an external or past-tense one. This is not a problem at all. In fact, the frequent shifting from external to internal (for example, through the use of TDS) has a useful fractionating effect. It also adds to the sense of frustrating the trance, meaning that the client is all the more eager to be 'released' into hypnosis.

## Why do you frustrate Trance?

The first time you encounter the Leisure Induction, the idea of delaying the moment your client goes into trance can seem counter-intuitive. Yet, this build up to the 'release' is one that I find particularly useful.

This may be more a matter of personal preference than anything else. However, there is no denying that when we are told we cannot have something, we want it all the more. In the same way, when you frustrate a desirable response in a subject, e.g. eye-closure, it makes it more compelling and ultimately irresistible.

As Stephen Brooks puts it, when discussing his use of this technique with a client, 'She can choose to take my suggestion to resist going into trance thereby making it more compelling, or she can choose to resist my suggestion to resist and so go into trance.'[7]

---

7 *Training in Indirect Hypnosis,* 1990, DVD, British Hypnosis Research, University of East Sussex.

**EXERCISE:**

Contact us at  www.howtodoinductions.com

if you have any ongoing questions which have not been answered.

GRAHAM OLD

# What Else?

## www.howtodoinductions.com

As you would expect, we would recommend our free inductions site as the premier website for learning about inductions.

Our web-site offers transcripts of various inductions, from the classics like Progressive Muscle Relaxation to the Bandler Handshake and others. New inductions are added - and annotated - regularly, but only after they have been assessed as useful and achievable for beginners and experts alike.

## www.briefhypnosis.com

Brief Hypnosis are the people behind *How to do inductions* and widely regarded as one of the 'go to' trainers of solution-focused hypnosis in the UK.

## Live Training

We also run live training in Therapeutic Inductions, offering hands-on experience in creating solution-focused inductions on-the-fly. You will learn principles and techniques that are not often taught elsewhere, which will take your confidence, creativity and client-base to new levels.

Sign-up for the newsletter at howtodoinductions.com to stay informed.

## Recommended Resources

*Training Trances* by John Overdurf & Julie Silverthorn

A record of a 4-day seminar provided by John Overdurf, *Training Trances* offers the reader a unique integration of Ericksonian techniques, traditional models of hypnotherapy and NLP. This must-have book includes numerous "live" demonstrations and a helpful chapter on revivification.

*Hypnotic Realities* by Milton Erickson

This unique book is the record of a demonstration by Milton Erickson of the art of inducing clinical hypnosis and indirect forms of suggestion. Includes detailed commentary by Erickson and Ernest Rossi.

*Training in Indirect Hypnosis* (DVD) by Stephen Brooks

This video demonstrates and dissects the innovative techniques of renowned hypnotherapist, Stephen Brooks. Not only does Brooks demonstrate the induction of indirect hypnosis, but he also evokes many of the classical hypnotic phenomena in an indirect and informal manner. This fascinating session was recorded at the University of East Sussex for inclusion in the British National Sound Archives.

*Clean Language* by Judy Rees & Wendy Sullivan

Clean Language is an elegant and powerful questioning technique that is remarkably simple to learn. Judy Rees and Wendy Sullivan show you how to get people to explore their internal metaphors, making it easier to understand them, motivate them or help them to change.

*Therapeutic Trances* by Stephen Gilligan

Gilligan presents what he calls 'the cooperation principle' and other fundamental elements of Ericksonian Hypnotherapy. Demonstrating how therapists can work with clients to translate problems into solutions, *Therapeutic Trances* includes helpful and extensive notes on the therapeutic use of trance and utilisation.

*Ericksonian Approaches* by Rubin Battino

*Ericksonian Approaches* is a comprehensive hands-on manual that offers a detailed overview of the nature, history, misconceptions and practice of Ericksonian hypnosis. A valuable and definitive work.

**EXERCISE**:

Continue to practice the Leisure Induction...

That's it!

Reading a book will not guarantee that you can make the most of this induction any more than a DVD on swimming will prepare you for the Sea.

Practice. Practice. Practice.

And then practice with a partner! Again and again and again...

Throughout your practice, focus on working with your client to assist them in to a deep experience of absorption in an experience they enjoy. Few people will object to this and it enables you to develop as a practitioner who empowers your clients for their own good.

# APPENDIX A – The Opening Question

There are a number of ways that you may want to ask the Opening Question, depending on where you are in a conversation and what you want to get out of it. You might be asking the question at the beginning of a therapy session, just to get to know someone. Or, you might be engaging in 'problem-free talk' at the beginning of a solution-focused therapy session, to ascertain resources and help someone shift their mindset into a more positive frame.

Alternatively, you may be carrying out formal hypnosis and be explicitly beginning an induction. Or, perhaps, you may simply be chatting to someone and wondering how easy it is to put into practice everything you've learned in this book.

I find it especially helpful to use the Leisure Induction at times when a client might seem 'stuck' in their problem, unable to take their mind off it, seemingly lacking hope or unsure what they want from therapy. At such times, it is a useful 'Therapeutic Induction.'

That means I am using the induction not merely to get someone 'under', or to get them into hypnosis so the real therapy can begin. The induction itself becomes a therapeutic process, where resources are uncovered, possibilities are explored and hope is re-ignited.

The following examples are genuine questions asked in therapeutic and non-therapeutic settings:

"So, what do you like to do when you're *not* working?"

"And if you could be doing anything you wanted right now...?"

"Tell me about the days when this problem isn't there."

"What kind of things do you do when you're happy?"

"What do you like to do to relax?"

"What's your favourite Leisure activity?"

"What hobbies or pastimes do you like to do?"

"How do you unwind?"

"What do you enjoy doing in your free time?"

"Tell me about a time when you found yourself doing something you were totally engrossed in..."

"Well, if I was to instruct you that you need to take some time for yourself, to just relax and do something enjoyable – almost like I'm putting it on a prescription as an essential part of your recovery! - what would you be doing?"

GRAHAM OLD

# APPENDIX B – Structural Variations

The following variations of the basic process are not offered as scripts to be bound by. However, we have noticed that some hypnotists struggle with the idea of a free-flowing conversation. They prefer to have more of a structure in mind.

For that reason, the following variations are offered as a framework that you may find helpful in your early experimentation with the Leisure Induction. Treat them like scaffolding, which provides useful security and stability when needed, but is never meant to be permanent.

These structures should be considered as guidelines, not directions.

So, if your client begins to 'go inside' from their very first answer, the last thing you should do is stop them because you are not yet at that stage!

Over time, you will most likely develop your own preferred approach, as you absorb the core principles and skills and allow yourself to flow with the process. Believe it or not, but this will be picked-up on by your clients, even if not consciously. The very way you ask your questions and feed back their answers will add to the fluid experience you are enabling them to re-live.

## A Simple Variation

1.     Describe 'naturalistic trance experiences', e.g. 'highway hypnosis', getting lost in a good book, etc.

2.     Ask if they have experienced anything like that.

3.     Ask the 5W & 1H questions to get the specifics: what, where, when, who, why and how.

4.     Use linking language to create fluid transitions

5.     Change from past tense to present

6.     Direct focus from external to internal

7.     Begin repeating verbal & non-verbal responses.

8.     As their minimal cues increase, tell them that when they cannot wait any longer they can close their eyes and slip into trance.

# MASTERING THE LEISURE INDUCTION

## A Present-tense Variation

1. Invite your client to tell you what they would be doing if they were currently taking part in their favourite leisure activity, or way to unwind.

2. Keep all of your questions and feedback in the present-tense.

3. Ask questions to gain more information.

4. Feedback their answers, particularly ones which you would want them to experience now, e.g. "you get comfortable..."

5. Progressively shift from an external focus to an internal one.

6. Feedback minimal cues as they occur, which assists with – and intensifies – the internalisation.

7. Eventually, give permission for them to fully enter into hypnosis.

## A Sensory Variation

1. Ask general questions about hobbies, life, pleasant experiences, etc.

2. Choose one of the answers that is associated with a 'dreamy' or trance-like experience.

3. Ask externally focused questions, primarilly using the sense of sight and hearing, e.g. "What can you see when you're playing Golf?", "Is anyone watching you?", "What do you hear?"

4. Feedback their answers throughout, especially any evocative, sensual or 'trancey' language.

5. Gradually begin to increase the amount of present-tense language. Using linkage words such as "as," "and," and "while" to create a smooth transition.

6. Ask any relevant questions about touch and taste? E.g. "And what does your body feel like as you prepare to take that shot?"

7. Continue to become more and more specific and move their attention inward to sensations, feelings and thoughts. Use feelings as the bridge from external to internal. E.g. "And what does that calm feel like?"

8. When you and your client are exclusively using internal and present-tense language, begin to change the sub-modalities of their experience.

9. Invite them to let go and drift fully into the experience now.

# MASTERING THE LEISURE INDUCTION

## A Direct Variation

1.    Enquire about the state of mind you want to evoke. E.g, "What is it like when you are totally absorbed in something?"

2. Tell them you are going to ask them to benefit from the power of their imagination, so invite them to close their eyes to assist with focus.

3.    Ask detailed questions about the answer you were given in #1.

4.    Tell them to step into their experience, "as if you were there now, seeing it through your own eyes."

5.    Continue to ask questions about their experience, in the present tense.

4. Use linking language to smoothly connect their replies. "So, your lying in your hammock in the Sunshine, what happens next?"

6. Feed answers back in the present tense, as embedded commands.

7. Shift the focus of your words from external descriptions of the setting and situation, to internal sensations and thoughts.

8. Use their nominalisations (used during #3 & #5) and pacing and leading to deepen their trance.

GRAHAM OLD

# APPENDIX C – Nominalisations

It can be helpful to think of nominalisations as words which allow people to add their own meaning. Or you might want to think of them as processes or verbs expressed as things or nouns.

For example, Communication is a nominalisation. Communication is not a 'thing' – you cannot put it in a wheelbarrow, after all. However, there is such an event as people taking part in communication.

The following list of nominalisations may help elucidate this point, as well as proving useful material for your practice of the Leisure Induction:

| | |
|---|---|
| Learnings | Relaxation |
| Clarity | Serenity |
| Curiosity | Fascination |
| Development | Decision |
| Integration | Leadership |
| Discovery | Relationship |
| Awareness | Confusion |
| Freedom | Maintenance |

Motivation

Openness

Fairness

Creativity

Enthusiasm

Honesty

Flexibility

Loyalty

Recognition

Satisfaction

Understandings

Knowledge

Nominalisation

Hope

Happiness

Contentment

Communication

Trance

Investigation

Courage

Continuation

Change

Desire

Resource

Transformation

Possibilities

Fulfilment

Realisation

Delight

Potential

Sensations

Exploration

# APPENDIX D - The Critical Or Analytical Client

Much has been written about the critical and/or analytical client. Newly-trained hypnotists and experienced Hypnotherapists can both become obsessed with trying to find out whether their client is critical or analytical, whatever that really means. Yet, since the day I was first taught the principles of the Leisure Induction, I have forgotten to worry about this issue, because this induction sidesteps any of those concerns.

Clients usually find the Leisure Induction an enjoyable experience, one which they happily go along with. Yet, it's still absolutely fine and normal for them to question the whole experience, whilst they are experiencing it. In fact I encourage it, if I think someone is showing signs that they will do this anyway.

A recent client of mine said, "I am really into this and its great, but my brain keeps going back to rationalise everything". In the spirit of mindfulness I said, "that's absolutely fine. Let your mind question it. And let the other part enjoy it as well. You don't need to get hung up about it. You can let those thoughts come in and go away again. Its all part of the process".

One of the reasons the Leisure Induction works so effectively is because we free the client to use their mind in an analytical way. However, before they have time to *over*-analyse and be critical, they are already in hypnosis. The reason this works is because we are using a personal experience the client has had that is non-threatening and enjoyable. There is no need to over-analyse or be critical of something you value and enjoy. Then, further into the induction, we can actually ask the client to analyse, identify and experiment with the feelings they have. So that part of their mind is satisfied and feels secure.

In fact, as we begin to feed-back the clients experience to them, their own analysis is actually part of what deepens the whole process for them.

The good news for us is that this means analytical clients often respond particularly quickly to the Leisure Induction – just another benefit!

# Bibliography

Bandler, R & Grinder, J. (1981). *Trance-formations: Neurolinguistic Programming and the Structure of Hypnosis.* Utah: Real People Press.

Battino, R & South, T. (2005). *Ericksonian Approaches: A Comprehensive Manual.* Carmarthen: Crown House Publishing.

Brooks, S. (1990). *"Training. in Indirect Hypnosis"* [DVD], University of East Sussex, British Hypnosis Research.

Chase, J. (2007). *Don't Look in His Eyes.* Devon: Academy of Hypnotic Arts.

Elman, D. (1964). *Hypnotherapy.* Glendale, CA: Westwood Publishing Co.

Erickson, M. H. (1976). *Hypnotic Realities: The Induction of Clinical Hypnosis and Forms of Indirect Suggestion.* New York: Irvington Publishers.

Gilligan, S. G. (1987). *Therapeutic Trances: The Co-Operation Principle In Ericksonian Hypnotherapy.* New York:

Routledge.

Korzybski, A. (1994). *Science and Sanity: An Introduction to Non-Aristotelian Systems and General Semantics.* New Jersey: Institute of General Semantics.

Nongard, R. (2007). *Inductions and Deepeners: Styles and Approaches for Effective Hypnosis*. Andover, KS: Peach Tree Professional Education.

O'Hanlon, W. H. (1987). *Taproots: Underlying Principles of Milton Erickson's Therapy and Hypnosis.* New York: Norton.

Overdurf, J & Silverthorn, J. (1995). *Training Trances.* Portland, OR: Metamorphouos.

Sullivan, W & Rees, J. (2008). *Clean Language: Revealing Metaphors and Opening Minds.* Carmarthen: Crown House Publishing.

Wiseman, R. (2010). *59 Seconds: Think a little, change a lot.* Oxford: Pan Books.

Yapko, M. (2003). *Trancework: An Introduction to the Practice of Clinical Hypnosis.* New York: Routledge.

# About the Author

**Graham Old** is a Solution-focused Hypnotist from the United Kingdom. A Graduate of Spurgeon's College, London and the University of Wales, Graham is a former University Chaplain and remains an active participant of local peace and justice campaigns. He also has experience as a Father's Worker and Assistant Social Worker, as well as working in private practice and running the most popular inductions site on the web.

Graham is a popular conference speaker, writer and trainer, with two decades experience teaching meditation and self-hypnosis. He is an innovative presence in contemporary hypnosis and the developer of the popular *Therapeutic Inductions* approach.

Made in the USA
Lexington, KY
16 August 2019